Great Lakes Wildlife

Includes:

Great Lakes Biomes

Habitats and Habits

Bird Activities

Mammal Activities

Reptile & Amphibian Activities

Invertebrate Activities

Wildlife Respect

Waterford Press

www.waterfordpress.com

Introduction

The Great Lakes is considered the largest group of freshwater lakes on Earth. The region surrounding the Great Lakes includes three major biomes—aquatic, grassland and forest. A biome is a large region that has similar plants, animals and organisms that have adapted to the geography and climate of that area. A biome can have several ecosystems.

An ecosystem is a community of organisms that interact with each other and with their environment. Several ecosystems can exist within a biome. Ecosystems within the three major biomes of the Great Lakes region include freshwater lakes, marshes, wetlands, dunes and prairies.

A diverse range of animals live in the Great Lakes region, including moose, bullfrogs, snapping turtles, eagles and a wide variety of fish species.

Great Lakes Biomes

Aquatic Biome

The aquatic biome of the Great Lakes includes five large, freshwater lakes—Lake Erie, Lake Huron, Lake Michigan, Lake Ontario and Lake Superior. More than 250 species of fish swim in the Great Lakes, including Atlantic salmon, northern pike, white perch and many others. Both native and introduced species live in the lakes, including the invasive zebra and quagga mussels, which live on lake bottoms.

Grasslands Biome

Dunes, wetlands and prairies are all part of the grasslands biome in this region. Grasses and shrubs are found on both stabilized and active sand dunes that form along the shores of the Great Lakes. Unstable (active) dunes are formed by windblown sand that is continuously moving. They have little vegetation but are sometimes covered by beach grass. Lakeplain wet prairie is a lowland prairie that occurs on the moist glacial lakeplains. Wetlands provide a safe place for many animals to nest while also helping to maintain water quality and prevent erosion on shorelines. Moose, beaver, river otter and coyote are some of the animals that call this area home.

Temperate Forest Biome

The Ottawa, Huron-Manistee, Hiawatha and Superior National Forests are a picturesque part of the Great Lakes region and provide habitats for many animals of the region. Hiawatha National Forest is also known as the Great Lakes National Forest. It receives almost 200 inches of snow each year. Ottawa National Forest is famous for its waterfalls. The Huron-Manistee is actually two forests but is managed as one. The Superior National Forest is as big as the three other national forests combined. It contains almost half a million acres of old-growth forest and the largest number of breeding birds of any national forest in the US.

Class Act

Animals can be sorted into categories based on certain characteristics. The system for sorting animals into categories is called taxonomy. Mammals, birds, fish, reptiles and amphibians belong to a class of animals called vertebrates. Vertebrates are animals with backbones. Invertebrates are another class of animals that do not have backbones (like insects, worms, clams and mussels).

Draw a line between the animal and its class.

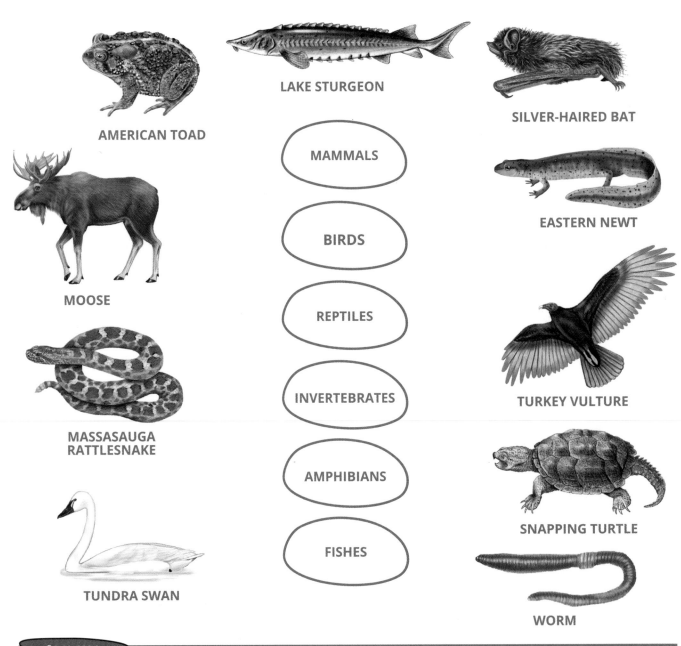

AMERICAN TOAD

LAKE STURGEON

SILVER-HAIRED BAT

MOOSE

EASTERN NEWT

MASSASAUGA RATTLESNAKE

TURKEY VULTURE

TUNDRA SWAN

SNAPPING TURTLE

WORM

MAMMALS

BIRDS

REPTILES

INVERTEBRATES

AMPHIBIANS

FISHES

You are What you Eat

Herbivores eat mostly plants. Carnivores eat other animals.
Omnivores eat plants and animals.

Draw a line between the animal and its diet.

RIVER OTTER

BADGER

DEER MOUSE

OMNIVORE

WHITE-TAILED DEER

HERBIVORE

COTTONTAIL

CARNIVORE

BLACK BEAR

WEASEL

WOOD DUCK

Food Chain

A food chain is the order in which animals feed on other plants or animals.

Producers – A producer takes the sun's energy and stores it as food.

Consumers – A consumer feeds on other living things to get energy. Consumers can include herbivores, carnivores and omnivores.

Decomposers – A decomposer consumes waste and dead organisms for energy.

Label each living organism below as a producer, consumer or decomposer.

CRAYFISH

_____

CATTAIL

_____

LYNX

_____

DUNG BEETLE

_____

WOOD DUCK

_____

WATER LILY

_____

Oddball Out

In each row, circle the animal that is different from the others.

1A | 1B | 1C | 1D

Three of these are herons; one is not.

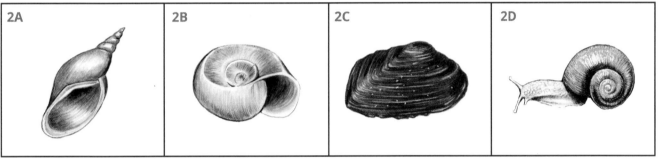

2A | 2B | 2C | 2D

Three of these are snails; one is not.

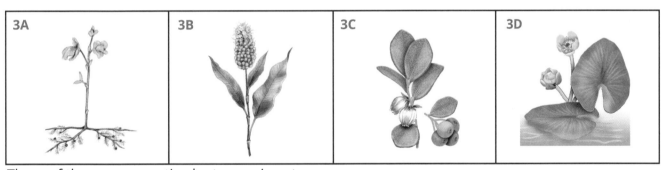

3A | 3B | 3C | 3D

Three of these are aquatic plants; one is not.

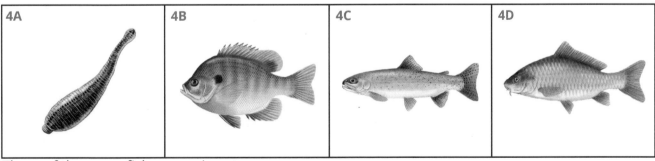

4A | 4B | 4C | 4D

Three of these are fishes; one is not.

Word Search

Ducks play an important role in ecosystems. As they swim, fly and feed, they introduce plant and animal species to new wetland areas by moving seeds, insect larvae and even frog eggs or fish from one place to another.

Find the names of these common ducks in the puzzle.

MALLARD

BLUE-WINGED TEAL

NORTHERN PINTAIL

```
N O R T H E R N S H O V E L E R
L O S Y B G L Z H X H X C K F P
A N R C J H T S L U W S R P W S
M O L T A F G S I J C P N G O A
E E W W H N Q X X W O N V G O H
R S J L P E V D R K G M B R D T
I J U G H T R A R E D H E A D T
C S W D P B Z N S G U V G X U S
A Z X T M V P J P B B M C S C N
N N H S C A G A A I A Q O F K A
W L Y O S K L V W Q N C Y K Q Z
I P O K N B S L G U W T K F J J
G P P J T P I Q A H T B A Z C H
E U A O L Q L W Q R C B L I T J
O B L U E W I N G E D T E A L M
N W F A U U R R S N I Y Z I J L
```

WOOD DUCK

CANVASBACK

REDHEAD

NORTHERN SHOVELER

AMERICAN WIGEON

Spot the Differences

Millions of birds migrate across the Great Lakes states to summer breeding grounds, resting and refueling along the way. Can you spot 10 differences between the images of these Great Lakes birds?

Answers

Color Me

The **cardinal**, a beautiful red songbird, is the official state bird of seven eastern states. The **wood duck** was celebrated by the Royal Canadian Mint with two special coins.

Use the color key to help you color these two distinctive birds of the Great Lakes.

CARDINAL

Color Key

WOOD DUCK

Color Key

Origami

The largest waterbird in North America, the trumpeter swan can be as tall as four feet with a wingspan of eight feet. Because it is so big, the trumpeter swan needs about 100 meters of open water to use as a "runway" when taking flight.

Starting with a square piece of paper, follow the folding instructions below to create a swan

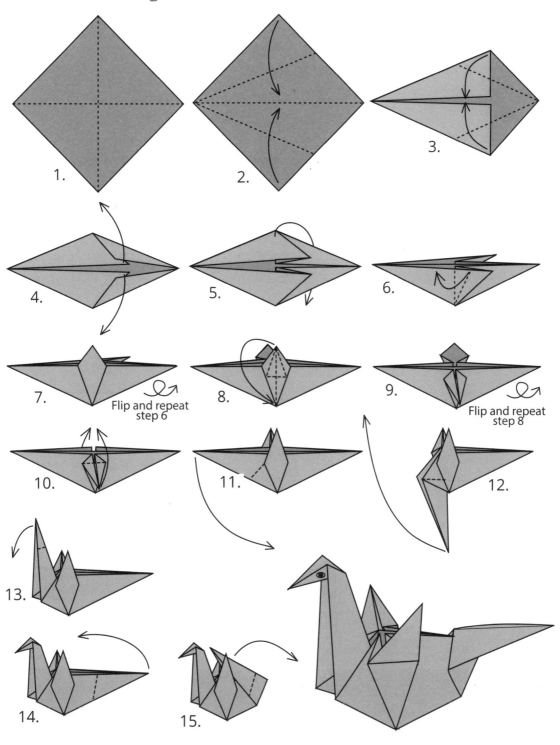

1.

2.

3.

4.

5.

6.

7.

Flip and repeat step 6

8.

9.

Flip and repeat step 8

10.

11.

12.

13.

14.

15.

Make Words

The **eastern meadowlark** is a beautiful, black and yellow grassland bird noted for its flute-like gurgling song.

How many words can you make from the letters in its name?

_____   _____

_____   _____

_____   _____

_____   _____

_____   _____

_____   _____

_____   _____

_____   _____

Maze

The **white-tailed deer** has a fluffy tail that is held erect when running. It can sprint up to 30 miles per hour, leap an 8-foot fence and jump a span of 30 feet in a single bound! The deer's size and speed are its defense from predators such as wolves, mountain lions and bears

Help this deer run away from the mountain lion.

ENTER

Word Search

A great number of mammals inhabit the Great Lakes area, including the little brown bat and river otter. The largest mammals include the moose, black bear, gray wolf and Canada lynx.

Find the names of these common Great Lakes mammals hidden within the puzzle.

WOODCHUCK

GRAY SQUIRREL

```
R F O U B Z M D M Q T W X D K A
W M H P Y S X P N Z Q F F D M K
B M K G U M L V S G T B L Q E P
Q I J X L X U H O R C T P F A O
B F X S T N R T K A A M F H D R
N I P T W B S Z C Y D C W C O C
W Y X R O O O I X F E T C H W U
S T L I B A O V T O E N M O V P
J N N P W O F D N X R K D C O I
N U T E H A E H C I M C R S L N
M X B D F Q Z C X H O G Y Q E E
M W O S G R A Y S Q U I R R E L
U R S K J M G F N B S C Q O I P
L R Z U S V F M Z P E W K I U E
N L Z N E C I L U A Y B R Q J Y
G N N K V B Z Z C P U F D U B J
```

RACCOON

MEADOW VOLE

PORCUPINE

GRAY FOX

Answers

STRIPED SKUNK

DEER MOUSE

14

Make Words

The **badger** is a fossorial animal. "Fossorial" means it is adapted to digging and lives mostly underground. It uses its long, front claws to dig in the ground to make a burrow and uses its back legs to kick out the dirt. It is known to dig faster than any mammal, including a man with a shovel. A badger usually dens in shallow burrows except during breeding season, when it will dig a nest chamber deep below the ground. The badger's black feet each have five toes, and the front feet have long, thick claws an inch or more in length. It has small eyes and ears and a slightly pointed nose. Its keen sense of smell is second only to that of members of the dog family.

How many words can you make from the letters in its name?

_____   _____

_____   _____

_____   _____

_____   _____

_____   _____

_____   _____

Answers

Possible words include: badge, barge, beard, grade, bread, aged, bead, bear, dare, dear, drag, drab, gear, grab, rage, read, bag, bed, beg, gab, rad, dab, are

15

Origami

The **Canadian lynx** is a medium-sized wild cat that lives in the Great Lakes region around Lakes Superior, Ontario and Huron. It is nocturnal, which means it is active at night, and it preys on snowshoe hares, birds and rodents.

Starting with a square piece of paper, follow the folding instructions to make this cat face. Decorate it to look like a Canadian lynx.

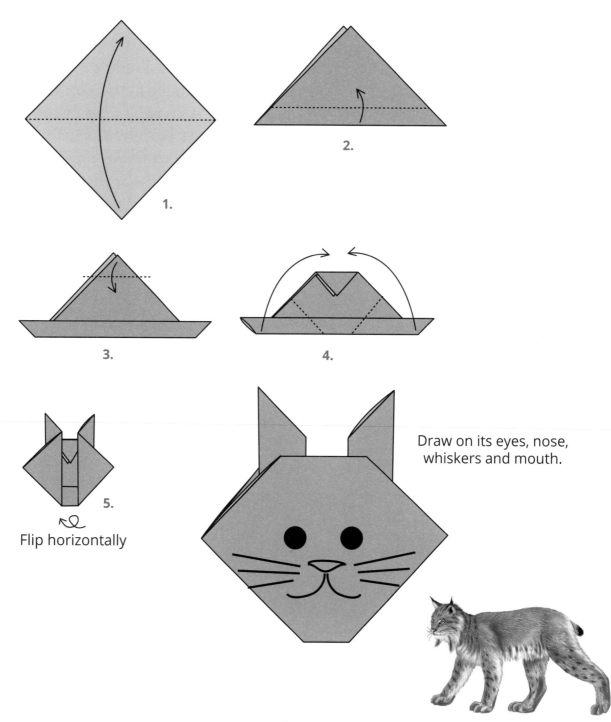

1.

2.

3.

4.

5.

Flip horizontally

Draw on its eyes, nose, whiskers and mouth.

16

Connect The Dots

This North American carnivore is named for its short, black-tipped, stubby tail. It inhabits a variety of habitats throughout the US, including the forests of the Great Lakes region. Its hind legs are longer than its front legs, so it walks with a bobbing motion.

Follow the numbers to connect the dots and reveal the mystery mammal

What am I?

Color Me

The **bluegill** is one of more than 250 species of fish that swim in the Great Lakes. It has flexible fins that give it the ability to reverse direction and even to swim backward!

Use the key to help you color this image of a bluegill.

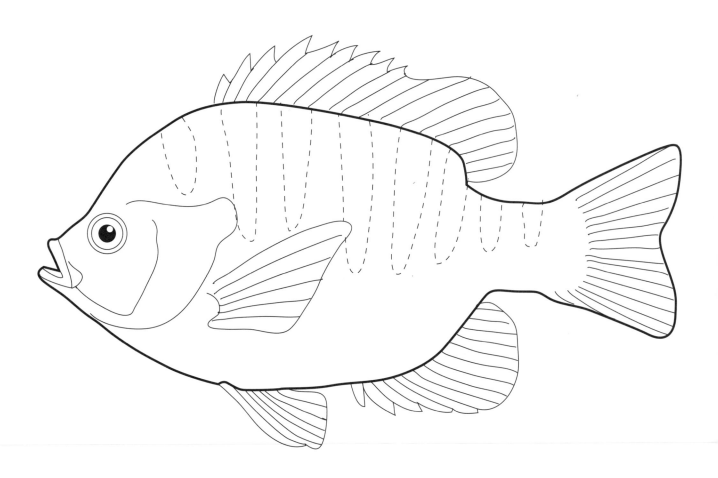

Color Key

Word Search

Find the names of these Great Lakes fishes.

LAKE TROUT

BROWN TROUT

YELLOW PERCH

WALLEYE

```
W B L A C K C R A P P I E K S L
W X C A X L B A J I A M D N X I
Q S Y A R R L O P M K H M W J Y
X L E M S G U Z Y U B I C C H D
W A L L E Y E O Z H R S M Y X U
D K L F X J G M N K O N E G F X
C E O Q J C I T O L W N K S M V
Z W W Z T P L N I U N E S A U L
M H P K R B L A K E T R O U T B
Y I E R A O G P T Y R H N Q Q D
S T R S D G C U J I O G B C W Y
V E C W Z L Q K I F U H X A G I
B F H E D K T N B H T N U P S V
I I D V U T S Q K A D E H E A S
I S P O K E N S W G S L X P C K
E H F X X P T N P E B S N G Q H
```

BLUEGILL

BLACK CRAPPIE

LAKE WHITEFISH

Answers

ROCK BASS

LARGEMOUTH BASS

19

Make Words

The **muskellunge**, also called the "muskie," is the largest member of the pike family. It can grow up to six feet long and up to 100 pounds. It is a voracious predator that feeds on fishes, ducks and amphibians.

How many words can you make from the letters in its name?

Answers

Possible answers include:
eel, elk, elm, emu, gel, gnu, gum,
leg, lug, men, mug, sue, sum,
sun, use, glue, glum, gull, gunk,
keen, knee, lung, menu, mule,
musk, sell, skull, smell, snug,
sunk, genus, lunge, sleek, slunk,
legume, sullen, unglue, ukulele

20

Color Me

There are four subspecies of **painted turtles** in the US—the eastern, midland, western and southern. Western painted turtles live on Lake Superior's shores, and midland painted turtles live north of Lakes Huron, Erie and Ontario. They like slow-moving waters and bays where they have plenty of plants to eat.

Use the key to color the image of the painted turtle.

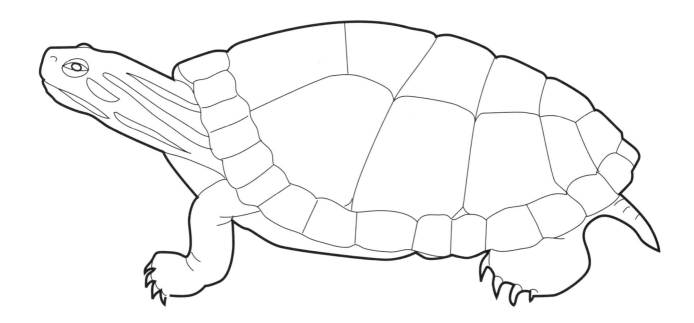

Color Key

Make Words

The **spring peeper** is a small frog that is easily identified by the dark X on its back. As its name implies, its call is a series of high-pitched peeps and is one of the earliest frog calls heard in spring. A chorus of these frogs has been compared to sleigh bells ringing. They are most often heard rather than seen since they live in dense vegetation.

How many words can you make from the letters in its name?

_____   _____

_____   _____

_____   _____

_____   _____

_____   _____

_____   _____

_____   _____

_____   _____

_____   _____

_____   _____

_____   _____

Connect the Dots

Bullfrogs are the largest frog species in the United States.
An adult can weigh over two pounds and be up to eight inches long.
Fun fact: The bullfrog can jump ten times the length of its body!

Follow the numbers to connect the dots and draw a picture of this amphibian.

Word Search

Amphibians are smooth-skinned, limbed vertebrates that live in moist habitats and breathe through lungs, skin, gills or a combination of all three. Frogs and toads are amphibians. Reptiles have dry, scaly skin and breathe air through their lungs. Snakes, lizards, turtles and tortoises are reptiles.

Find the names of these reptiles and amphibians in the puzzle.

PAINTED TURTLE

SNAPPING TURTLE

MASSASAUGA

```
I G Y L T I O V Q E E T C V P V
M W A T E R S N A K E X R V I W
Y I S Y B N N D Q D S A A C O T
O S N P O M P F D Q M F V H A Y
G E A F R K A K L R U U H O G D
B L P Z B I I S O G B J Y R A C
K R P W L V N H S G X F B U R V
J F I E O C T G Q A C I N S T X
F Y N I P O E Z P C S U G F E E
C H G G K C D I Q E S A E R R L
H J T V W S T F U I E K U O S E
K W U Q E E U I R C U P I G N P
G O R O J P R W S O F V E N A I
F E T I F C T Q I Z G I T R K B
P F L R X B L A V N Q V X Q E T
O G E L A S E D A A D S B C Y U
```

SKINK

CHORUS FROG

WOOD FROG

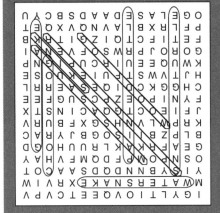

Answers

SPRING PEEPER

WATER SNAKE

GARTER SNAKE

24

Be an Artist

North America has 327 **dragonfly** species. Dragonflies and their smaller relatives, the damselflies, belong to the order Odonata, which comes from the Greek word for "tooth." The Hine's emerald dragonfly, found scattered throughout the Great Lakes region, is known for its bright green eyes, and is one of the most endangered dragonflies in North America

Draw this dragonfly by copying one square at a time.

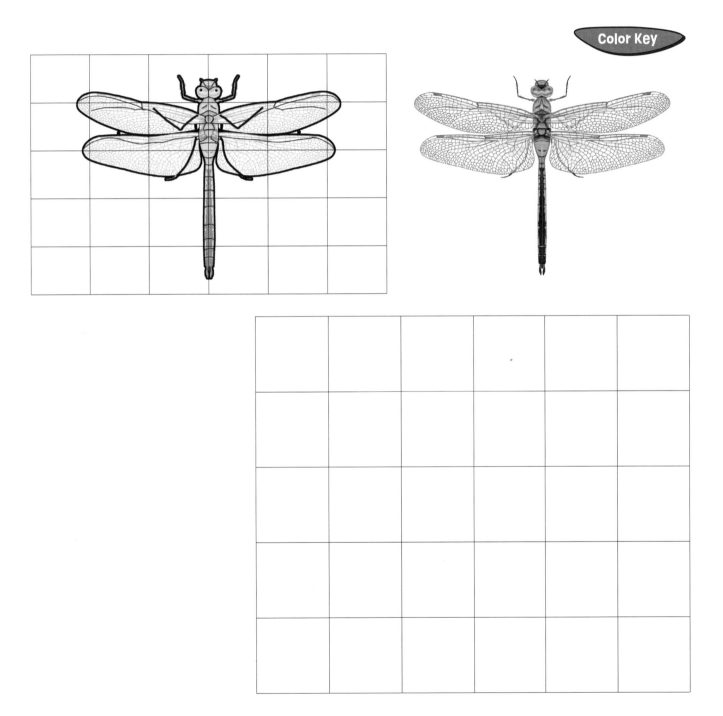

Color Key

Origami

Starting with a square piece of paper, follow the simple folding instructions below to create a dragonfly.

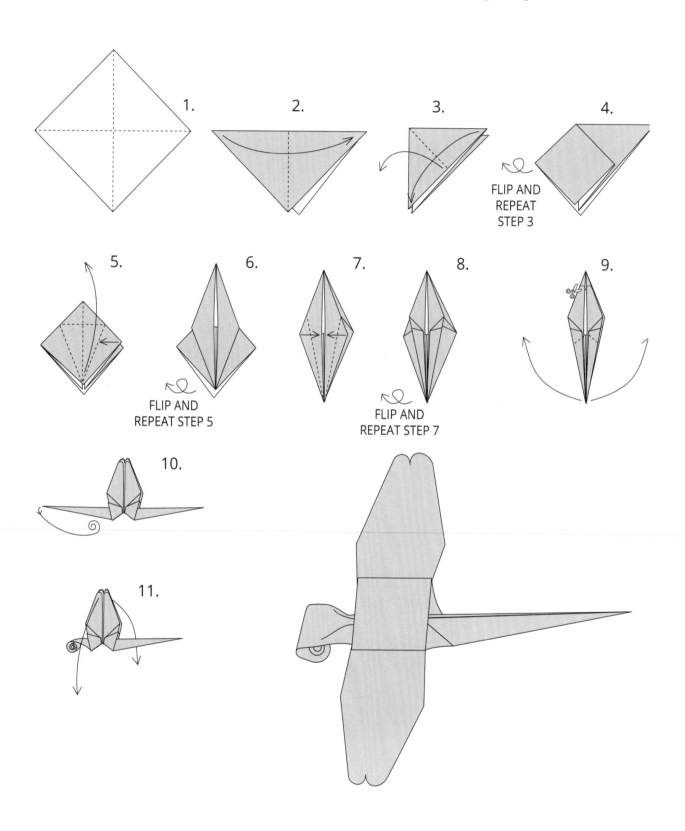

Maze

The **green darner** is one of North America's most common dragonflies. It has a bright green chest (thorax) and a blue body. It is one of the largest dragonflies with a body length and wingspan of about 3 in. (8 cm). It is often seen in the vicinity of ponds and waterways, resting on plants with it wings spread open.

Help this green darner find the mosquito.

ENTER

Be an Artist

Draw this backswimmer by copying it one square at a time.

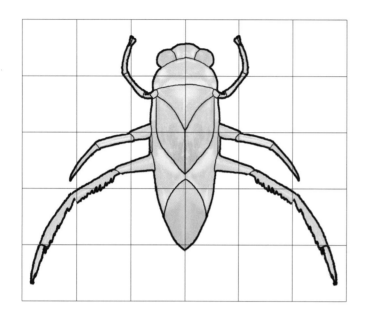

Backswimmers are aquatic insects that swim across the surface of ponds on their backs, using their bristly legs as oars. They are predators and feed on other invertebrates and even tadpoles and small fish. They can inflict a painful bite, so be careful not to handle them.

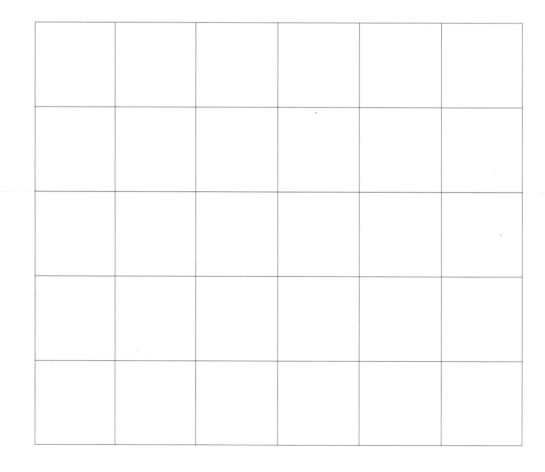

Color Key

Who Am I?

Insects represent 60% of all life on Earth and are a very important part of the animal kingdom. The diversity of the environment in the Great Lakes, from freshwater to wetlands to forests and shorelines, makes for a large number of insect species. When winter comes, some insects seek shelter underground or in logs or trees. Some, like the honeybee, huddle together for warmth.

Draw a line between the Great Lakes insect and its name.

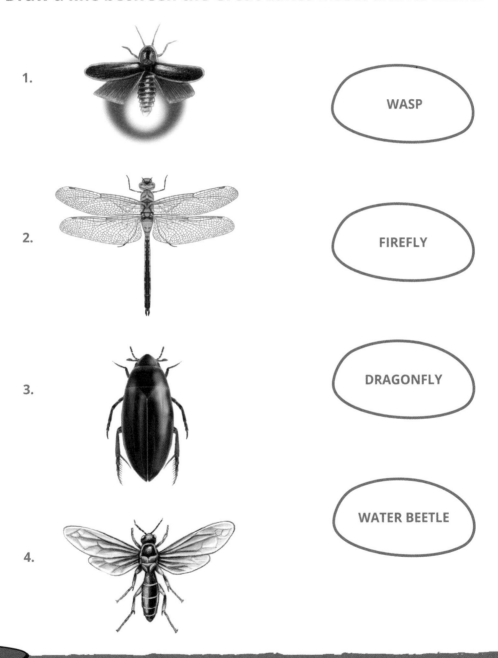

1.

WASP

2.

FIREFLY

DRAGONFLY

3.

WATER BEETLE

4.

Connect the Dots

Over 1,000 species of butterflies and moths have been identified in the Great Lakes region due to the many types of habitats. One of them, the giant swallowtail, is the largest butterfly in North America.

Draw this prairie butterfly as it feeds on pollen and nectar from grassland wildflowers

Word Search

The forests, wetlands, lake shores, dunes and plains of the
Great Lakes are home to more than 270 species of wildflowers.

Find the names of these Great Lakes wildflowers in the puzzle.

```
R D N R V V X C X Z X T O B G U
D W S D S T Q K U T Z N I T U Q
Z B A M X O J Z Z R W I K N F Z
J Z L T E N U Z K O S I D M Z L
T X O A E P V F Z U S D M J M L
R G C L C R Q A X T V J C D F Z
I N O A O K L R S L K S C Y K X
L G L G W X E I L I H L T W L W
L I U Q V E E Y L L N R Y A Z U
I L M X E C D Y E Y F U O G P C
U I B D T J H D E D V X F J Z U
M T I Z C T T X N D S X M K F F
B U N C H B E R R Y A U L M M Y
J N E U K O K E E Y O I S Z J Y
G F V E X X J O Y M Z R S A I K
T O P L N D U S O W D T B Y N P
```

COW VETCH

TROUT LILY

TRILLIUM

**BLACK-EYED
SUSAN**

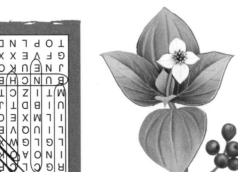

OX-EYE DAISY

COLUMBINE

BUNCHBERRY

WATER LILY

Answers

```
T O P L N D U S O W D T B Y N P
G F V E X X J O Y M Z R S A I K
J N E U K O K E E Y O I S Z J Y
B U N C H B E R R Y A U L M M Y
M T I Z C T T X N D S X M K F F
U I B D T J H D E D V X F J Z U
I L M X E C D Y E Y F U O G P C
L I U Q V E E Y L L N R Y A Z U
L G L G W X E I L I H L T W L W
I N O A O K L R S L K S C Y K X
R G C L C R Q A X T V J C D F Z
T X O A E P V F Z U S D M J M L
J Z L T E N U Z K O S I D M Z L
Z B A M X O J Z Z R W I K N F Z
D W S D S T Q K U T Z N I T U Q
R D N R V V X C X Z X T O B G U
```

31

Wildlife Respect

In wild spaces, humans are the visitors. We are lucky to be able to observe animals in their natural habitats. Along with that privilege, comes a responsibility to respect the animals we see, as well as their homes. The best way to learn about wildlife is by quietly watching. Though the possibility of getting a better look—or a better photo—can be tempting, getting too close can be stressful to a wild animal.

Here are some ways you can help reduce the number of disruptive human encounters that wild animals experience:

1. Know the site before you go.

2. When taking photos, do not use a flash, which can disturb animals.

3. Give animals room to move and act naturally.

4. Visit after breakfast and before dinner when wild animals are less active.

5. Do not touch or disturb the animals.

6. Do not feed the animals.

7. Store your food and take your trash with you.

8. Read and respect signs.

9. Do not make quick movements or loud noises.

10. Report any encounters with dangerous animals.